Capturing *the* EXPERIENCE

My child's first year in college

A parent's memory journal of the child's first year in college

COPYRIGHT 2018, 2017 by Pinecrest Street Company

All rights reserved. This publication is protected by Copyright laws. No part of this book may be reproduced, stored in a retrieval system, or transmitted in any form, or by any means electronic, mechanical, photocopying, recording, or otherwise with prior permission of Pinecrest Street Company, and as expressly permitted by the applicable copyright status. Dissemination or sale of any part of this book is not permitted. Request for written permission may be obtained by writing Pinecrest Street Company, LLC. 11301 S. Dixie Hwy. Box 5666684, Miami FL 33256.
Pinecrest Street Company crest is a trademark of Pinecrest Street Company, Inc. and is registered in the United States.
ISBN 978-0-9995575-7-0

Executive Editor: Carlos Borges
Authors: Kay Lopate and Patsy Self Trand
Book Design and Layout: Ana Garcia and Alexa Behm
Published independently by Pinecrest Street Company, LLC.
www.pinecreststreetcompany.com
Address 11301 S. Dixie Hwy. Box 566684 Miami FL 33156
Printed in the United States

Books Published by Pinecrest Street Company, Inc.

College Bound Series: Knowing What to Expect – Preparing for "A's"

30 Awesome reading and learning strategies for high school students. (2017). Trand, Patsy Self and Lopate, Kay. Pinecrest Street Company.

Become a great college reader: Get the basics of reading now before you begin college. Book 1. (2017). Lopate, Kay and Trand, Patsy Self. Pinecrest Street Company.

Getting the basics of critical thinking for college readers and writers. Book 2. (2018). Lopate, Kay and Trand, Patsy Self. Pinecrest Street Company.

Challenge Series: Success in Difficult Courses – Making "A's"

Making it to Graduation: Expert advice from college professors (2nd, ed.) (2018). Lopate, Kay and Trand, Patsy Self. Pinecrest Street Company.

The Official Parent Playbook: Getting your child through college. (2nd, ed.) (2018) Lopate, Kay and Trand, Patsy Self. Pinecrest Street Company.

Making it in Medical School: Expert advice from college professors. (2019). Lopate, Kay and Trand, Patsy Self. Pinecrest Street Company.

Making it in Nursing School: Expert advice from college professors. (2019). Trand, Patsy Self, and Lopate, Kay. Pinecrest Street Company.

The athletes' playbook for college success. (2018). Trand, Patsy Self and Lopate, Kay. Pinecrest Street Company.

Vocabulary university professors say that every college student should know. (2017). Trand, Patsy Self and Lopate, Kay. Pinecrest Street Company.

Navigating Through College and Beyond Series – Making more "A's"

Capturing the Experience: My child's first year in college. (2nd,ed.) (2017) Lopate, Kay and Trand, Patsy Self, Carpenter, Sara, Pinecrest Street Company.

Capturing the Experience: My first year in college. (2nd,ed.) (2017) Lopate, Kay and Trand, Patsy Self, Carpenter, Sara, Pinecrest Street Company.

Reading and Learning the Required College Courses in the Historical and Social Sciences. Book 3. (2017). Trand, Patsy Self and Lopate, Kay. Pinecrest Street Company.

Reading and Learning the Required College Courses in the Biological and Mathematical Sciences. Book 4 (2017). Trand, Patsy Self and Lopate, Kay. Pinecrest Street Company.

30 Amazing reading and learning strategies for college students. (2017). Lopate, Kay and Trand, Patsy Self. Pinecrest Street Company.

Why I didn't come to class. (2018). Trand, Patsy Self and Lopate, Kay. Pinecrest Street Company.

PINECREST STREET COMPANY, LLC.
Pinecrest Street Publishing
www.pinecreststreetcompany.com
Pinecrest Street Company, LLC
11301 S. Dixie Hwy. POBox 566684
Pinecrest, FL 33256

You've made it!

Congratulations! Your child is now leaving home for college. All the new experiences and events that will occur for both you and your child this year are too precious to forget. You will want to capture and record as much as you can about this momentous year and this book is fun and efficient way to do it!

Years from now you will enjoy reading about the significant memories and the emotions you felt at that time. You will delight in recalling the feelings of excitement, joy and pride as well as the sadness you felt as you left your child at college.

This is an opportunity to record your feeling and create a lasting keepsake. Don't let this important year slip by without preserving the memories of your child's first year in college and the changes in your life. These are memories that should never be forgotten!

After completing this record you may choose to share it with your child, save it as a family keepsake, or retain it as a memoir.

Write a letter
TO YOURSELF

__ / __ / __
(Date)

Dear _____,
      (parent's name)

It has been about _____ since you left for _____
               (number of days or weeks)

_____ located in _____.
(name of school)

_____ gave me this book to recall all my feelings
(name of person)

and thoughts about your first year in college.

I know this freshman year is going to be like no other year. I'm hoping to complete all the sentence prompts in this memory book because I want to preserve in writing all the exciting things that will happen to you and our family this year.

At this time I feel _____. If I were to
               (describe your feelings after your child has
               been in college for about a week)

choose 3 words to describe the way you are right now, they would be _____, _____, and _____.

A few things that surprised me about the college you are attending are _____ During your freshman year, I predict you will become more _____ and less _____. There will probably be changes in our family as well. I forsee some of those changes might be _____. We miss you very much and look forward to _____.

Best wishes and much love,

                            _____
                            (your name)

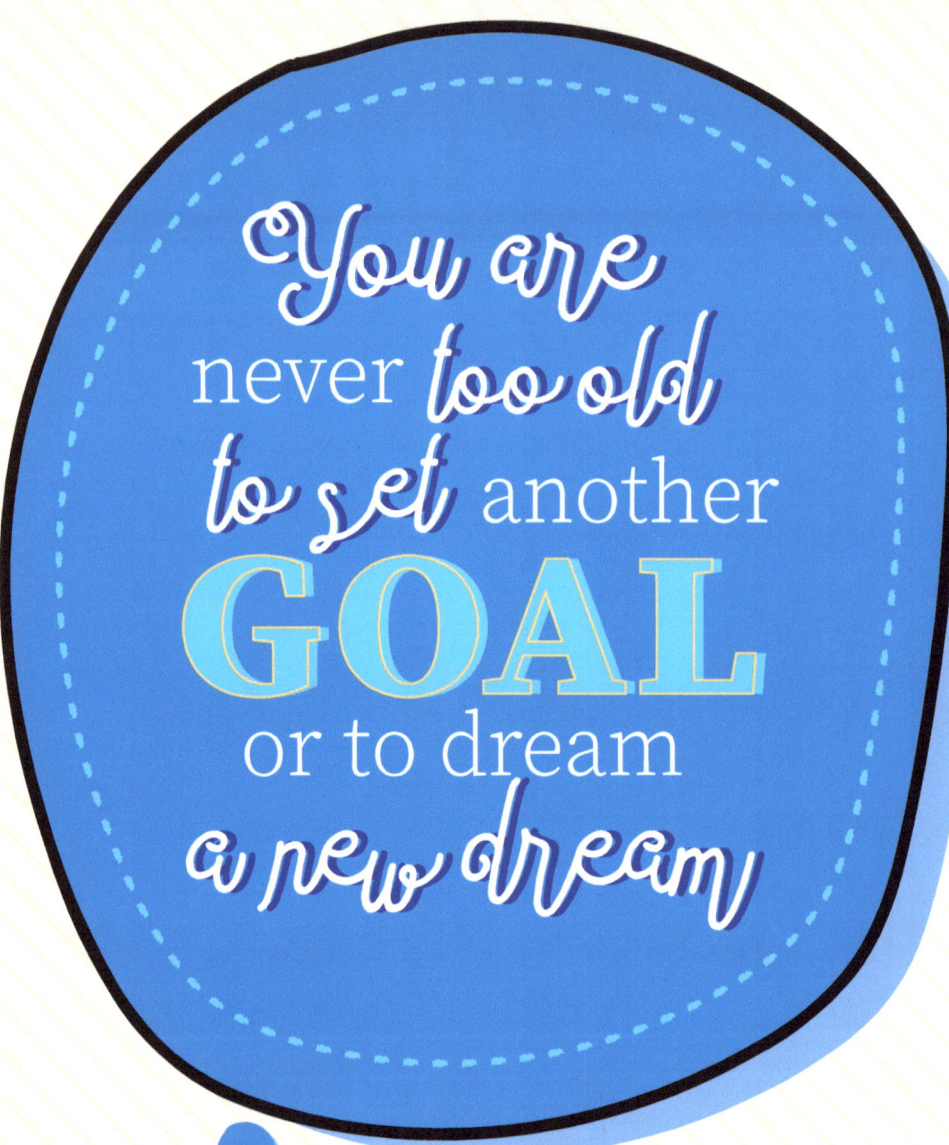

FIRST Semester

_____ to _____

✕ ✕ ✕
My first impression of the college campus was

✗ ✗ ✗
A few things that surprised me about the college campus were

✕ ✕ ✕
My reaction to your dorm room was

x x x
The one thing I should have told you before you left was

My first impression of your roommate was

✕ ✕ ✕
Here is how I felt when we said goodbye

___

✕ ✕ ✕

After you left home, the first time I went into your room, I

× × ×
My thoughts about "letting go" are

The realization that you are now a college student makes me feel

✕ ✕ ✕
I try to compensate missing you by

Although it is your choice, I wish you would consider majoring in

I'm hoping you have met people you consider friends because

✗ ✗ ✗
In the first care package I send you, I plan to include

✖ ✖ ✖
My thoughts regarding the major you have chosen are:

✗ ✗ ✗
While you are away at school, I will miss going with you to

✕ ✕ ✕
On your first college break, I imagine you will

✕ ✕ ✕
Since you left for school, the changes in my grocery shopping are

✕ ✕ ✕
I love being your parent because

✕ ✕ ✕
The changes in meal planning and housekeeping are

Memories

Glue a picture here

TICKET STUBS

TRAVELS

ANECDOTES

Glue a picture here

Glue a picture here

✗ ✗ ✗
If I were to enroll in college, I would

✕ ✕ ✕
Some things about college that I question are

✗ ✗ ✗
Since you left for college, our house is

I know you have your own goals, but a few goals
I'm hoping you also have are:

✕ ✕ ✕
Before you left for college, I wish I had taught you how

✗ ✗ ✗
Now that I have more time and I can go anywhere for a weekend, I will go

Memories

Glue a picture here

TICKET STUBS

TRAVELS

ANECDOTES

Glue a picture here

Glue a picture here

✗ ✗ ✗
I feel that the biggest fear you may have is

___

___

___

___

___

___

___

___

___

___

___

___

___

The first time you return home on break, I will prepare your favorite food including

I am looking forward to your being home this first semester. Some things I am planning are:

✗ ✗ ✗

I plan to send you an email with words of encouragement as you study for final exams, I will be sure to say

Memories

Glue a picture here

TICKET STUBS

TRAVELS

Glue a picture here

ANECDOTES

Glue a picture here

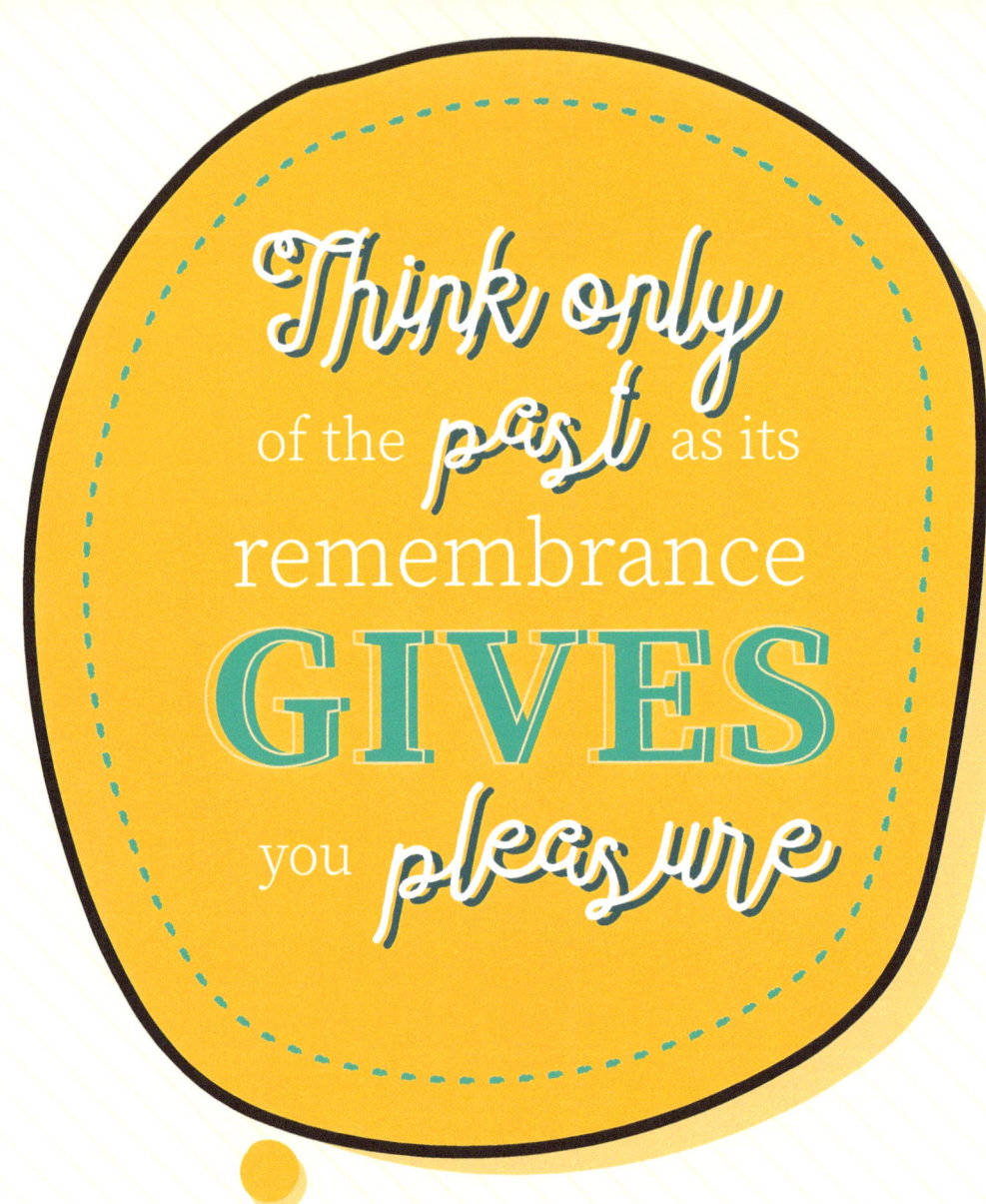

SECOND Semester

_____ to _____

x x x
The thing I miss most about you is

× × ×
When you leave for college this time, I am

✕ ✕ ✕
After spending time with you, I've noticed that you seem

✗ ✗ ✗
Having you back home was

x x x
While you were home on break, I feel that the nicest thing you and I did together was

TICKET STUBS

TRAVELS

ANECDOTES

× × ×
At this time, I am looking forward to

✗ ✗ ✗
Some things on my current wish list are

✕ ✕ ✕
I love being your parent because

✗ ✗ ✗
Some changes I will make to the house while you are away are:

✕ ✕ ✕
Some new and different things I hope to do while you are away are:

✕ ✕ ✕
I imagine one day you will be living in

✗ ✗ ✗
I recently saw an old photo of you and

✕ ✕ ✕
It was difficult for me to realize that

X X X

I enjoy remembering the time when we

× × ×
The one thing about you that I hope never changes is

Memories

Glue a picture here

TICKET STUBS

TRAVELS

ANECDOTES

Glue a picture here

Glue a picture here

✕ ✕ ✕
When I think about the future, I envision that you will become

_____

_____

_____

_____

_____

_____

_____

_____

_____

_____

_____

_____

_____

✕ ✕ ✕
If I were given one million dollars today I would

✗ ✗ ✗
The change in you I like the most since becoming a college student is

✕ ✕ ✕
Some of the many other changes about you I have noticed since you started college are

✗ ✗ ✗
I hope you never forget

✘ ✘ ✘
The way you've managed money in college has been

✕ ✕ ✕
I thought I would never be able to

✖ ✖ ✖
I stay positve doing

✕ ✕ ✕
I like spending Sundays

✗ ✗ ✗
I am confident you will be succesful because

✕ ✕ ✕
As college student, the way you now dress is

✕ ✕ ✕
Some advice I plan to give you when this semester is over is

✗ ✗ ✗
Some advice I would like to give you but probably don't have the courage to give is

✗ ✗ ✗
I'm hoping you will spend our summer doing these things:

✕ ✕ ✕
My thoughts regarding where you will be living after you graduate from college

✕ ✕ ✕
A few things about you that I hope never change are

TICKET STUBS

TRAVELS

Glue a picture here

ANECDOTES

Glue a picture here

Write a letter
TO YOURSELF

_____ / _____ / _____
(Date)

Dear _____,
         (your name)

Wow! You have just completed your first year of college! I feel
_____
         (describe your feelings)
_____
         (describe your feelings)

I've noticed you have changed in a few ways. The changes I've observed about you are _____
_____.

I have changed in a few ways. Now I am more _____
_____.

This summer I expect you will be _____
_____.
      (list the activities you think your child will be doing)

I haven't received your grades yet but I expect they will be _____
_____. Next year I imagine your plans will be
(your estimation of grades earned)
_____.
      (your child's plan for next semester)

As I look back over these past two semesters, I think that this year has been _____.
      (use one or two adjectives that summarixe this year)

      Love,

                                   _____
                                    (your name)

www.ingramcontent.com/pod-product-compliance
Lightning Source LLC
Chambersburg PA
CBHW042323150426
43192CB00001B/29